ENDLESS EMOTIONS

A Collection Of Poems

Bishal Kumar Bhuyan, Jina Moni Upadhyaya & Shubham Bhowmick

Printed and bound in India

Title: Endless Emotions
Language: English
Character set encoding: UTF-8

First published by

An Imprint of BlueRose Publishers

Head Office: B-6, 2nd Floor,
ABL Workspaces, Block B, Sector 4,
Noida, Uttar Pradesh 201301
M: +91-8882 898 898

BlueRose ONE .com
Stories Matter
DIY

We, the Poets, with love and respect dedicated this book

'Endless Emotions' to our Families.

ACKNOWLEDGEMENTS

My dear readers, thanks to you for picking up this book of poetry, Endless Emotions where we, the poets, mainly reflects on the emotions, the sentiments of those who feel strongly at different phases of life. Thank you for your love & blessings.

Perhaps Endless Emotions would not been released without the support of you, Aditya, Sifa, Shubham & Jina. I honestly expresses my gratitude for your feedbacks & edits.

I am extremely thankful for my family members & friends for your kind help & Co-operations in my writings.

And lastly, thanks BlurRose, for giving me the platform for Publication.

CONTENTS

1. GLEAM AND SHINE

The fluttering time soars
And doesn't look on your gores
You have mounted up, reached desirable shore
Why can't then walk up a little more
The sky always remains in far to revive
But droplet of rain touches us to keep live
The sun always pops up to bright the earth
The stygian night always comes to heal us
Our wounds leave scar
To mend it we have to roam afar
To gleam and shine
Walk forward from the darkest line
You are not only enduring alone
Everyone is putting energy to glint like a moon.

-Jina Upadhyaya

2. NEVER HAVE I IMAGINED

Never have I imagined
That we would fall in love
Never have I imagined
That we would kiss each other.
Never have I imagined
That you will turn me on
Never have I imagined
That I'll give you all my heart.
Never have I imagined
That you would break me apart
Never have I imagined
That I would leave your heart.
Never have I imagined
That I'll suffer so much
Never have I imagined
That love would painful so much.
Never have I imagined
That you'll hide things from me
Never have I imagined
That you'll cheat on me
All that I understand,

All that I know is now,
That I was never yours,
And you were never mine.
- **Bishal Kumar Bhuyan**

3. LIFE

Life is a feel that we dont care,
We just walk through the path,
And associate ourself with some fear.
There is no place in this world,
To hide from our own situations,
Some day we will have to face them ,
And face some humility,
But it doesnt matter,
How much we hear.
Only the thing is that,
Wjat outcome we bring out from there,
For every situation,
We have to bring something new,
And tackle the problem,
That we are going through,
In every step someone is waiting to humiliate,
And bring out our mistake,
To pull us back there will be many hands,
But we have to fight,
Only with two hands,
No one else is going to stand for us,

No is going to raise their voice for us,
Only they can do is to criticize,
Ignoring them we have to,
move forward with a raging heart.
- **Shubham Bhowmick**

4. FLEE WITH TIME

The puffy air blown, As if it made a way near to my arms

My hairs came to my face and my cheeks were fraught, my eyes were ill at ease

My hands were trying to bring a comfortable zone

For all the parts of me

But my segments were muttering, I can see

Albeit, I tried thousands of time

To bring the earlier vibes of sublime

My legs slipped even if the street was not slippery or stonyfield

It was just metaphor which showed the wield

I did every possible things to make happy each of my segments

But always somewhere somehow something were lost

I was in great distress and exhaust

The wind again appeared and blown

With greater power now it had shown

Now hairs were already in between stings of ribbon

And my cheeks were benign, eyes were merrily glisten

Sedately, I begin to put things where it belongs
I lose my treasure sometime
And I learnt new lesson to flee with time.
- **Jina Upadhyaya**

5. NO ONE CAN ERASE YOUR DREAMS

The whereabouts of our respective journey
Indeed seems prolong and never ending
The road often gives you warmness with full of beans
And often strong blow comes to seed spleen
Tears and woes become inseparable
Eyes become swollen over night like incurable
And next day again your heart will wrap up
Slowly you will learn to accept all the challenges
And your six sense will be ever ready for next
Your core will carry so much bandages
But then become stronger than ever
Now when hard storm knocks you
You would be happy to face it
Cause it will teach you new lesson
And you will discover new ideas to solve
No one can beat you down
Unless you beat up yourself
No one can hurt you again
Unless you allow them

No one can finger your choices
Unless you surrender yourself
No one can erase your dreams & yearning
Unless you stop fighting and capitulate
- **Jina Upadhyaya**

6. MOTHER, I FEAR

Mother I fear of losing you!
What if something were to happen to you?
Mother, I fear, if you leave me behind,
How will I live, the answers I can't find!
Mother I fear, if you leave me behind,
I know not what consequences shall unwind!
Mother I fear if I were orphaned,
I will be threatened or murdered!
Mother I fear, if were orphaned,
They'll start taking me for granted!
If such happens, I would rather die.
Please think of me!
Please don't make my cry!
- Bishal Kumar Bhuyan

7. ESSENCE OF FAILURE

Essence of success, you never tasted
Sweetness of luxor you will never get
Every piece of work you ever did
Came up with a bold failure list
But you never got defeated
And always tried to correct your mistake
You never ran behind success
But you are running before your mistakes
Every time you think
How to remain undefeated
From the challenges you face everyday.
- **Shubham Bhowmick**

8. RANK GROUPERS

People around ignores my presence
Just because I am not a spunk
Why is it necessary ?
To be popular
Is it not enough to be good
Everyone has a basic need.
To go with the person of good deeds.
But its not true in real sense.
Everyone runs behind money and fame
Why is it not enough to be good?
Why is it necessary to be in a group
Someone run behind the ranks .
Someone run behind the status.
But what about those
Who lies in between of those
people in the world juy7
Has some unique in their nature .
No one can get anyone ,
Having similar desire ,
For someone it is easy to fix ,
But for others it is beyond their reach ,

No one can understand the pain of failures .
Just they stick behind the so called rank holders
.

- Shubham Bhowmick

9. STAY STRONGER

Times are tough,
But we are tougher.
The phase is dark,
But we are warrior.
Hope is there,
If we stay stronger.
Angels are there,
To protect and guide us here.
Stay stronger
Fight light a deadly fighter
To become a winner
- Bishal Kumar Bhuyan

10. YOU ARE LEAVING

You are going
And I haven't met you.
You are leaving
And I haven't seen you.
Yet we have tackled
Many Situations,
Overcome
Many Difficulties.
Haven't imagine that,
Destiny will bring Separation.
Haven't imagine that
How strange this Life is.
- Bishal Kumar Bhuyan

11. PURE LOVE

The rains are so romantic,
As if blessings to pure love.
Everything seems so magical and pure,
When you're in love.
Drops of rain starts singings,
Washing away the grime,
the mistakes and the crime.
Feeling the void in my life,
With love so pure so bright
Dancing in the rain with you,
Feels so delightful
as if entering an unfathomadle world,
Where each drop of rain
Tells me
To claim your breath.

- Bishal Kumar Bhuyan

12. FAITH REVITALIZES LIFE

The long walks make strong triumph
The hardest paths make dizzy highest
Life is a colossal rebelling sea
As well as dazzle illuminating tree
Life brings unpredictable blocks
Along uncountable aching slots
We often break and fall in the ground
To rouse again seems onerous sound
To control your self from melancholy
Have to seed the faith of revitality
Believe over oneself is only the cure
The impossible tackles resolve forsure
Today's reality is self centered being
We often forget, all are same mortal living
Albeit no one is coming forward to see
You are the only source to revive your glee
Your ascendancy over pessimism
Also lights up your surrounding's optimism
Trust build slowly over the time
Things take time to mend it's totally fine
Make a vast move as a lion's soar

Your faith will revitalize yourself more and more.

- **Jina Upadhyaya**

13. NATURE'S PLAY

Life changes people changes
Only words remain in this world
For eternal times
Nothing is immortal here
Except the thought of the fickle mind
People say we born again
But who knows ?
What the nature does with the consciousness
Weather we take birth or
We mix up with the natural essence
Only we can get the present moments .
That we don't get twice
Leaving everything we are running behind attaining nirvana
But what is the benefit of doing so
When we don't even know that
What is the mystic law of nature
So live how much you can
Breathe how much you can contain
Because we never know
Who is gonna stay till

We reach the living fair
- **Shubham Bhowmick**

14. EASY ON YOURSELF

The wonders of unfathomable mind
Brings whirl of angst confined
Muddle up/confused brain cells
Where the starter & where the ends
There's so much to say
And trying to find somehow a way cause lips are closed
Some uneasy things has exposed
To pour down the latent of the heart
The frozen part to melt & cease
Exhausted still gesturing to reimpose
The things which are meant to bloom like rose
Gracious & easy on the eye
Still people dare to touch her allies
Lets give a try to flow, having thorns also beauty to glow
Immense blowing thought
Painful scares have already taught
Do love, lap up & be easy on yourself
And never allow to throw things of your shelf.

- **Jina Upadhyaya**

15. FASCINATION

Holding my earbuds
Listening to the EDM hits.
Increases the thrill in me
And makes me realize that.
How much its important
To express our emotions
To those about whom we really care .
Now I believe that rather than
Smoking a puff of cigarette
And having a shot of vodka
Don't relieve us from pain.
But a women with a caring heart
Can make a man realize
The value of life.

- Shubham Bhowmick

16. MY LOVE

My Love, the moment I saw you
Everything Paused, Everything Halt.
You became my strength, my weakness.
You are now my everything, my world.
You are my love, my rhythm.
My heart beats for you, my love.
You are mine and I am yours!
You are in my soul, you are in my heart,
You are in my each breath.
I exist only for you,
Without you I am dead.
- **Bishal Kumar Bhuyan**

www.ingramcontent.com/pod-product-compliance
Ingram Content Group UK Ltd.
Pitfield, Milton Keynes, MK11 3LW, UK
UKHW022007190726
13853UKWH00004B/1796